EMMANUEL JOSEPH

Navigating the Emotional Journey: A Guide to Divorce Recovery"

Copyright © 2023 by Emmanuel Joseph

All rights reserved. No part of this publication may be reproduced, stored or transmitted in any form or by any means, electronic, mechanical, photocopying, recording, scanning, or otherwise without written permission from the publisher. It is illegal to copy this book, post it to a website, or distribute it by any other means without permission.

First edition

This book was professionally typeset on Reedsy. Find out more at reedsy.com

Contents

1	Understanding Divorce as a LifeTransition	1
2	The Emotional Rollercoaster of Divorce	4
3	Grieving the Loss of Your Marriage	7
4	Coping with Anger and Resentment	10
5	The Importance of Self-Care during Divorce	13
6	Rebuilding Your Self-Esteem and Confidence	16
7	Communicating Effectively with Your Ex	19
8	Co-Parenting with Compassion and Cooperation	22
9	Dating and Relationships After Divorce	25
10	Financial Recovery and Planning for the Future	28
11	Legal and Practical Considerations	31
12	Embracing a New Beginning: Thriving After Divorce	34

1

Understanding Divorce as a Life Transition

Introduction:
Divorce is often described as the death of a marriage, and like any significant loss, it can trigger a wide range of emotions. In this chapter, we will explore the concept of divorce as a life transition and delve into the emotional journey that accompanies it. Understanding the nature of divorce is the first step towards navigating this challenging period in your life and ultimately finding a path to recovery and healing.

1.1 The Nature of Divorce:
Divorce is the legal dissolution of a marriage, but it is also a profound life transition. It marks the end of a significant chapter in your life and the beginning of a new one. It's crucial to recognize that divorce is not solely about legal proceedings or property division; it's a complex emotional and psychological process.

1.2 The Emotional Impact:
Divorce often brings forth a whirlwind of emotions. You may experience grief, anger, sadness, confusion, guilt, or even relief. It's entirely normal to feel a mixture of these emotions, and they can fluctuate over time. Understanding

that these emotions are a natural response to a major life change is the first step in coping with them effectively.

1.3 The Stages of Divorce Grief:

Many experts compare the emotional journey of divorce to the stages of grief described by Elisabeth Kubler-Ross. These stages include denial, anger, bargaining, depression, and acceptance. While not everyone experiences these stages in the same way or order, they provide a framework for understanding the emotional ups and downs of divorce.

1.4 The Importance of Self-Compassion:

During divorce, it's easy to be hard on yourself, blaming yourself for the end of the marriage or feeling inadequate. Self-compassion is a vital concept to embrace. It means treating yourself with kindness and understanding, just as you would a close friend going through a tough time. Self-compassion is the cornerstone of emotional healing.

1.5 Seeking Support:

You don't have to go through divorce alone. Seek support from friends, family, or a therapist who specializes in divorce recovery. Support groups can also be immensely beneficial, as they provide a safe space to share experiences and learn from others who are on a similar journey.

1.6 Setting Realistic Expectations:

Understanding that divorce recovery is a process that takes time is essential. There is no set timeline for healing, and everyone's journey is unique. It's crucial to set realistic expectations for yourself and recognize that healing and rebuilding your life will happen at your own pace.

Conclusion:

Divorce is a significant life transition that brings emotional challenges, but it's also an opportunity for personal growth and a fresh start. By understanding the nature of divorce and the emotional journey it entails, you are better equipped to navigate this difficult period. In the chapters that follow, we will explore strategies and tools to help you move forward on your path to divorce recovery.

2

The Emotional Rollercoaster of Divorce

Introduction:
Divorce is an emotional rollercoaster, with highs and lows that can leave you feeling disoriented and overwhelmed. In this chapter, we will explore the various emotions you may encounter during the divorce process, how to cope with them, and ways to regain emotional stability.

2.1 Emotions in Flux:
Divorce triggers a wide range of emotions, and they often come in waves. One day you may feel a sense of relief or even hope, while the next may bring intense sadness or anger. Recognizing that these emotions are part of the process can help you navigate them more effectively.

2.2 Grief and Loss:
At the heart of divorce is the loss of a significant relationship. Grief is a natural response to this loss, and it can manifest in various ways. You might mourn the loss of companionship, shared dreams, or the life you once had. It's essential to allow yourself to grieve and not rush through this important emotional process.

2.3 Managing Anger and Resentment:
Anger is a common emotion during divorce, whether directed at your

ex-spouse, the situation, or even yourself. It's crucial to find healthy ways to manage and express this anger, such as through therapy, journaling, or physical activity. Holding onto resentment can hinder your healing process.

2.4 Coping with Loneliness:
Divorce often leads to a sense of loneliness and isolation. You may miss the daily companionship and support of your spouse. It's essential to reach out to friends and family for social support during this time. Additionally, consider joining support groups or seeking professional help to combat loneliness.

2.5 Navigating Confusion and Uncertainty:
Divorce can bring about a sense of confusion and uncertainty about the future. You may be unsure about financial stability, living arrangements, or co-parenting arrangements. Developing a clear plan and seeking legal advice when necessary can help alleviate some of this uncertainty.

2.6 Embracing Moments of Hope:
Amidst the emotional turmoil, there will be moments of hope and optimism. These moments may be fleeting, but they serve as reminders that healing and personal growth are possible. Embrace these moments when they come and use them to fuel your journey toward recovery.

2.7 The Importance of Emotional Self-Care:
Self-care is crucial when navigating the emotional rollercoaster of divorce. Ensure that you prioritize your physical and mental well-being. Activities like exercise, meditation, therapy, and spending time with loved ones can help you maintain emotional stability.

Conclusion:
The emotional rollercoaster of divorce can be challenging, but it's a natural part of the process. By acknowledging and understanding the various emotions you may experience, you can better cope with them. In the upcoming chapters, we will explore specific strategies and techniques to

help you navigate these emotions and move forward on your path to divorce recovery.

3

Grieving the Loss of Your Marriage

Introduction:
Grief is an inevitable companion on your journey through divorce. In this chapter, we will delve deeply into the grieving process, examining the stages of grief, the unique aspects of grieving a marriage, and practical ways to navigate this emotional terrain.

3.1 The Uniqueness of Grieving a Marriage:
Grieving the end of a marriage is distinct from other forms of grief. It involves not only the loss of a partner but also the loss of shared dreams, routines, and a way of life. Recognizing this unique form of grief is essential for understanding your emotional journey.

3.2 The Stages of Grief:
Elisabeth Kubler-Ross's stages of grief—denial, anger, bargaining, depression, and acceptance—provide a framework for understanding your emotional responses to divorce. It's important to note that these stages are not linear and may be experienced in a different order or repeated.

3.3 Denial:
Denial is often the first emotional response to divorce. It can manifest as disbelief or a sense of numbness. You may find yourself questioning if the

divorce is real or hoping for reconciliation. Acknowledging denial is the first step in moving through it.

3.4 Anger:
Anger can be directed at your ex-spouse, yourself, or even the situation itself. It's crucial to find healthy ways to express and manage anger, as unresolved anger can hinder the grieving process.

3.5 Bargaining:
During this stage, you may find yourself making deals or "what if" scenarios in your mind. You might wish you had done things differently or that the marriage could have been saved. Recognize that bargaining is a normal part of the process, but it may not change the outcome.

3.6 Depression:
Depression in the context of divorce often involves deep sadness, loss of interest in activities, and feelings of hopelessness. If you find yourself stuck in this stage, seeking professional help can be beneficial to address your emotional well-being.

3.7 Acceptance:
Acceptance doesn't mean you're happy about the divorce, but it signifies a degree of emotional resolution and a willingness to move forward. It's important to note that acceptance may come and go, and that's okay.

3.8 Honoring Your Grief:
Allow yourself to grieve fully and without judgment. Grief has no timeline, and everyone's experience is unique. Give yourself permission to mourn the end of your marriage and the life you had envisioned.

3.9 Coping Strategies:
Seeking support from friends, family, or a therapist can be instrumental in navigating grief. Create rituals or memorialize the positive aspects of your

marriage that you'd like to carry forward. Journaling and creative outlets can also help you process your emotions.

Conclusion:

Grieving the loss of your marriage is a crucial step on the path to divorce recovery. It's a process that takes time and patience. By understanding the stages of grief and finding healthy ways to navigate them, you can honor your emotional journey and begin to heal from the profound loss of your marriage.

4

Coping with Anger and Resentment

Introduction:
 Divorce often stirs up intense emotions, and anger and resentment are two of the most common ones. In this chapter, we'll explore the nature of anger and resentment during divorce, their impact on your well-being, and effective strategies for coping with and eventually letting go of these powerful emotions.

4.1 The Role of Anger and Resentment:
 Anger is a natural response to the upheaval and pain that divorce can bring. You may feel angry at your ex-spouse, the circumstances that led to the divorce, or even yourself. Resentment can develop as a result of holding onto unresolved anger over time. These emotions can be consuming, but they can also be managed.

4.2 Understanding Your Anger:
 To cope with anger effectively, it's crucial to understand its root causes. Is it directed at a specific event, ongoing conflicts, or a sense of injustice? Identifying the source of your anger can help you address it more directly.

4.3 Expressing Anger Safely:

Suppressing anger is unhealthy, but expressing it in destructive ways can lead to further complications. Seek healthy outlets for your anger, such as talking to a therapist, confiding in a trusted friend, or channeling your emotions into physical activities like exercise or hobbies.

4.4 Forgiveness and Letting Go:
Forgiveness is a powerful tool for releasing anger and resentment. It doesn't mean condoning harmful actions or reconciling with your ex-spouse. Instead, forgiveness is a gift you give yourself to free your heart from the burden of carrying grudges.

4.5 Self-Compassion:
Practice self-compassion by acknowledging that it's okay to feel anger and resentment during this challenging time. Be kind to yourself and avoid self-blame. Self-compassion can create space for healing and personal growth.

4.6 Setting Boundaries:
Establishing clear boundaries with your ex-spouse can help minimize ongoing conflicts and reduce opportunities for anger and resentment to fester. Effective communication and clear agreements can be essential in this regard.

4.7 Seeking Professional Help:
If anger and resentment are overwhelming and persistent, consider seeking the assistance of a therapist or counselor who specializes in divorce recovery. They can provide strategies for managing these emotions and offer a safe space to explore their underlying causes.

4.8 Focusing on the Future:
While it's essential to acknowledge and work through anger and resentment, it's also vital to shift your focus toward the future. Consider setting new goals, nurturing your personal growth, and visualizing a life beyond divorce.

Conclusion:

Coping with anger and resentment during divorce can be challenging, but it's a crucial part of your emotional healing journey. By understanding the origins of these emotions, expressing them safely, and practicing self-compassion and forgiveness, you can gradually free yourself from the grip of anger and resentment. This process allows you to reclaim your emotional well-being and move forward on the path to divorce recovery.

5

The Importance of Self-Care during Divorce

Introduction:
Divorce can be emotionally draining, and it's easy to neglect self-care when you're focused on the practical and emotional challenges of the process. In this chapter, we'll explore the significance of self-care during divorce, its positive impact on your well-being, and practical strategies for self-nurturing.

5.1 Defining Self-Care:
Self-care encompasses a wide range of practices and habits that prioritize your physical, emotional, and mental health. It's about taking deliberate actions to nurture and care for yourself during difficult times, such as divorce.

5.2 Why Self-Care Matters:
During divorce, it's common to put the needs of others before your own, but neglecting self-care can lead to burnout, increased stress, and compromised emotional well-being. Engaging in self-care practices is essential for maintaining resilience and navigating divorce with greater ease.

5.3 Physical Self-Care:

Physical self-care involves taking care of your body. This includes getting regular exercise, maintaining a balanced diet, getting enough sleep, and attending to any medical or healthcare needs. Exercise, in particular, can release endorphins and help alleviate stress.

5.4 Emotional Self-Care:

Emotional self-care is about recognizing and addressing your emotions. Practice self-compassion by allowing yourself to feel and express your emotions without judgment. Consider journaling, meditation, or therapy to explore your feelings and gain emotional clarity.

5.5 Mental Self-Care:

Mental self-care involves stimulating your mind positively. Engage in activities that challenge and stimulate your intellect, such as reading, learning a new skill, or pursuing a creative hobby. Mental stimulation can help divert your focus from the challenges of divorce.

5.6 Social Self-Care:

Maintaining social connections is vital during divorce. Spend time with friends and loved ones who provide emotional support and understanding. Isolation can intensify feelings of loneliness and sadness, so make an effort to stay connected.

5.7 Practical Self-Care:

Practical self-care includes managing the logistical aspects of life. Ensure you attend to financial responsibilities, legal matters, and any co-parenting agreements promptly. A sense of control over these aspects can reduce stress and anxiety.

5.8 Setting Boundaries:

Learn to set boundaries with others, including your ex-spouse and well-meaning friends and family. Protect your time and emotional energy by communicating your needs and limitations clearly.

5.9 Daily Self-Care Rituals:

Incorporate daily self-care rituals into your routine, no matter how small. These rituals can act as anchors of stability during turbulent times. Whether it's a morning meditation, a daily walk, or a moment of gratitude, these practices can foster resilience.

Conclusion:

Self-care is not a luxury but a necessity during divorce. By prioritizing self-care in all its forms—physical, emotional, mental, social, and practical—you can build a foundation of resilience that will help you navigate the challenges of divorce more effectively. Remember that taking care of yourself is not selfish; it's a vital part of the divorce recovery process.

6

Rebuilding Your Self-Esteem and Confidence

Introduction:
Divorce can take a toll on your self-esteem and confidence. In this chapter, we will explore the impact of divorce on your self-image, the importance of rebuilding your self-esteem, and practical strategies to regain your confidence and sense of self-worth.

6.1 The Impact of Divorce on Self-Esteem:
Divorce can shatter your self-esteem. Feelings of rejection, failure, and self-doubt often accompany the end of a marriage. It's crucial to recognize these emotions and their impact on your self-image.

6.2 Self-Esteem vs. Self-Confidence:
Self-esteem refers to your overall sense of self-worth and self-acceptance, while self-confidence is your belief in your abilities and judgments. Both are interconnected, and rebuilding one often helps bolster the other.

6.3 Challenging Negative Self-Talk:
Start by becoming aware of negative self-talk and self-criticism. Challenge these thoughts by examining their validity and replacing them with more

positive and self-affirming beliefs.

6.4 Self-Compassion:
Practice self-compassion by treating yourself with the same kindness and understanding you would offer a close friend facing a difficult situation. Remember that you are not defined by your divorce.

6.5 Setting Realistic Goals:
Rebuilding self-esteem and confidence is a gradual process. Set realistic goals for yourself and celebrate your achievements, no matter how small. Each step forward is a victory.

6.6 Self-Care for Self-Esteem:
Engage in self-care practices that promote self-esteem, such as regular exercise, a balanced diet, and adequate sleep. Physical well-being can have a significant impact on how you perceive yourself.

6.7 Building New Skills and Interests:
Exploring new interests or rekindling old ones can boost your self-esteem. Learning a new skill, pursuing a hobby, or setting personal challenges can provide a sense of accomplishment and pride.

6.8 Seeking Support:
Lean on your support network, including friends, family, and therapists, to help rebuild your self-esteem. They can provide encouragement, positive reinforcement, and a listening ear during moments of self-doubt.

6.9 Professional Help:
If rebuilding your self-esteem and confidence feels particularly challenging, consider seeking therapy or counseling. A therapist can provide specialized guidance and strategies tailored to your needs.

6.10 Embracing Your Individuality:

Remember that your identity is not solely defined by your role as a spouse or ex-spouse. Embrace your individuality and focus on your unique qualities, strengths, and values.

Conclusion:

Rebuilding your self-esteem and confidence after divorce is a vital aspect of your journey toward recovery. By challenging negative self-perceptions, practicing self-compassion, setting achievable goals, and seeking support, you can regain your sense of self-worth and confidence. Embrace the opportunity for personal growth and self-discovery that divorce can offer, and know that you have the resilience to rebuild and thrive.

7

Communicating Effectively with Your Ex

Introduction:
Effective communication with your ex-spouse is essential, especially if you share children or have ongoing financial or legal matters to address. In this chapter, we will explore strategies for navigating communication with your ex-spouse in a way that minimizes conflict and promotes cooperation.

7.1 The Importance of Effective Communication:
Open and respectful communication can significantly reduce stress and conflict during and after divorce. It's a vital skill for co-parenting, resolving issues, and moving forward with your separate lives.

7.2 Setting Clear Boundaries:
Establish clear boundaries for communication with your ex-spouse. Define how, when, and under what circumstances you will communicate. Having these boundaries in place can help prevent misunderstandings and conflicts.

7.3 Use Neutral and Respectful Language:
Choose your words carefully when communicating with your ex-spouse. Use neutral and respectful language, and avoid blame, criticism, or accusations. Remember that your goal is to find solutions, not assign blame.

7.4 Active Listening:

Practice active listening when your ex-spouse is speaking. Give them your full attention, ask clarifying questions, and validate their feelings and concerns. This can create an atmosphere of mutual respect.

7.5 Keep Emotions in Check:

It's natural for emotions to run high during divorce-related discussions. However, try to keep your emotions in check when communicating with your ex-spouse. If a conversation becomes too heated, consider taking a break and returning to it later when you are both calmer.

7.6 Use Written Communication:

For important matters or when emotions are particularly sensitive, consider using written communication, such as emails or text messages. This can provide a record of your discussions and allow you to carefully consider your responses.

7.7 Co-Parenting Plans:

Develop a clear and detailed co-parenting plan that outlines schedules, responsibilities, and guidelines for raising your children. Having a written agreement can minimize disagreements and provide a framework for your co-parenting relationship.

7.8 Mediation or Therapy:

If communication with your ex-spouse remains challenging, consider enlisting the help of a mediator or therapist specializing in co-parenting or divorce communication. They can facilitate discussions and provide strategies for improved communication.

7.9 Parallel Parenting:

In cases of high conflict, parallel parenting may be necessary. This approach involves minimizing direct communication and interactions with your ex-spouse and focusing solely on essential matters related to your children.

7.10 Focus on the Future:

Remember that the goal of communication with your ex-spouse is to address practical issues and ensure the well-being of your children, not to rehash past conflicts. Keep your discussions future-oriented and solution-focused.

Conclusion:

Effective communication with your ex-spouse is a challenging but crucial aspect of post-divorce life, especially if you have children. By setting clear boundaries, using respectful language, practicing active listening, and seeking outside help when needed, you can create a more cooperative and constructive co-parenting relationship. Effective communication ultimately benefits not only you and your ex-spouse but also the well-being of your children.

8

Co-Parenting with Compassion and Cooperation

Introduction:
Co-parenting after divorce can be a complex and emotionally charged endeavor. In this chapter, we will explore the principles of co-parenting with compassion and cooperation, fostering a healthy and supportive environment for your children during and after divorce.

8.1 The Importance of Co-Parenting:
Co-parenting is about working together with your ex-spouse to provide a stable and nurturing environment for your children. It plays a pivotal role in helping children adjust to the changes brought about by divorce.

8.2 Put Children First:
Make your children's well-being the top priority in co-parenting. This means setting aside personal conflicts and differences to ensure that your children have the love, support, and stability they need.

8.3 Consistent and Clear Communication:
Open, consistent, and clear communication with your ex-spouse is vital for successful co-parenting. Share important information about your children's

schedules, activities, and well-being. Use a shared calendar or communication app if necessary.

8.4 Coordinating Parenting Styles:
While you and your ex-spouse may have different parenting styles, aim for consistency in rules and expectations between households. This helps provide a sense of stability for your children.

8.5 Flexible Scheduling:
Recognize that flexibility is key in co-parenting. Be open to adjustments in schedules and arrangements to accommodate your children's needs, school events, and extracurricular activities.

8.6 Resolving Disagreements:
Disagreements with your ex-spouse are inevitable. When they arise, approach them with a problem-solving mindset. Consider mediation or therapy to help find compromise and resolution.

8.7 Create a Parenting Plan:
Develop a detailed parenting plan that outlines custody arrangements, schedules, responsibilities, and guidelines for decision-making. A well-structured plan can reduce confusion and conflict.

8.8 Respect Boundaries:
Respect personal boundaries between households. Avoid intruding on your ex-spouse's time with the children unless it's an emergency or agreed upon in advance.

8.9 Avoid Negative Talk:
Refrain from speaking negatively about your ex-spouse in front of your children. Negative talk can create confusion, stress, and loyalty conflicts for them.

8.10 Self-Care for Co-Parents:

Take care of your own physical and emotional well-being. Co-parenting can be challenging, and you'll be better equipped to support your children if you're emotionally healthy.

Conclusion:

Co-parenting with compassion and cooperation requires effort and dedication, but it's one of the most valuable gifts you can give to your children after divorce. By prioritizing your children's needs, maintaining open communication, and working together with respect and flexibility, you can create a supportive co-parenting relationship that fosters the emotional well-being and resilience of your children.

9

Dating and Relationships After Divorce

Introduction:
After divorce, many individuals contemplate dating and forming new romantic relationships. In this chapter, we will explore the complexities of dating and relationships post-divorce, offering guidance on when and how to approach this aspect of your life with intention and self-care.

9.1 The Decision to Date Again:
Deciding to date after divorce is a highly personal choice. Take the time to evaluate your emotional readiness and consider factors such as your children's well-being, your own healing process, and your desire for companionship.

9.2 Self-Reflection:
Engage in self-reflection to gain clarity about what you're seeking in a new relationship. Reflect on your past marriage, the lessons learned, and the qualities you value in a partner.

9.3 Healing and Self-Care:
Before entering a new relationship, focus on your own healing and self-care. Ensure that you are emotionally resilient and capable of approaching dating with a healthy perspective.

9.4 Communicating with Your Children:

If you have children, communicate openly and age-appropriately about your decision to date again. Be prepared for their reactions, which may include confusion, anxiety, or resistance.

9.5 Taking It Slow:

When you do decide to date, take it slow. There's no rush, and it's essential to build a foundation of trust and compatibility with a potential partner.

9.6 Redefining Relationships:

Understand that post-divorce relationships can look different from what you've experienced in the past. Be open to redefining your expectations and priorities in a partner.

9.7 Online Dating:

Online dating can be a convenient way to meet new people, but exercise caution and prioritize safety. Take time to get to know potential partners before meeting in person.

9.8 Honesty and Transparency:

Honesty and transparency are crucial in new relationships. Be open about your divorce and any relevant details with your potential partner.

9.9 Handling Rejection:

Rejection is a part of dating, and it can trigger emotions related to your divorce. Learn to cope with rejection by reframing it as an opportunity for growth and self-discovery.

9.10 Balancing Dating and Co-Parenting:

If you're co-parenting, balance your dating life with your responsibilities to your children. Ensure that your children's needs remain a top priority and that dating doesn't disrupt their routine or stability.

Conclusion:

Dating and forming new relationships after divorce can be both exciting and challenging. Approach this phase of your life with self-awareness, self-care, and a commitment to your own emotional well-being. By taking the time to heal, being transparent with potential partners, and maintaining balance with your parenting responsibilities, you can navigate dating and relationships after divorce in a way that aligns with your personal growth and happiness.

10

Financial Recovery and Planning for the Future

Introduction:
   Divorce often has significant financial implications that require careful consideration and planning. In this chapter, we will explore the steps and strategies for achieving financial recovery after divorce and planning for a stable and secure future.

10.1 Assessing Your Financial Situation:
   Begin by assessing your current financial situation. Gather information on your assets, debts, income, expenses, and financial obligations resulting from the divorce.

10.2 Creating a Budget:
   Develop a comprehensive budget that reflects your post-divorce financial reality. This budget should cover your everyday expenses, savings goals, and any support payments or alimony arrangements.

10.3 Financial Independence:
   Work toward financial independence. This may involve finding employment if you're not already employed or advancing your career to increase

your income.

10.4 Property and Asset Division:

Understand the legal aspects of property and asset division in your divorce settlement. Ensure that you receive your fair share of assets and that your financial interests are protected.

10.5 Alimony and Child Support:

If applicable, know your rights and obligations regarding alimony and child support. Ensure that support agreements are in line with legal guidelines and your financial capabilities.

10.6 Establishing New Financial Accounts:

Separate joint financial accounts and establish new ones in your name. This helps create financial autonomy and prevents complications related to shared accounts.

10.7 Debt Management:

Develop a plan for managing any shared debts from your marriage. Consider consolidating or refinancing loans to make payments more manageable.

10.8 Saving and Investing:

Prioritize saving and investing for your future. Set up an emergency fund, contribute to retirement accounts, and explore investment opportunities that align with your financial goals.

10.9 Estate Planning:

Update your estate plan to reflect your post-divorce wishes regarding inheritance, beneficiaries, and the distribution of assets in case of your passing.

10.10 Seek Professional Guidance:

Consult with a financial advisor or planner who specializes in divorce recovery. They can help you navigate complex financial decisions and create a long-term financial plan.

Conclusion:

Financial recovery after divorce is a critical component of rebuilding your life. By assessing your financial situation, creating a budget, working toward financial independence, and seeking professional guidance, you can regain financial stability and plan for a secure future. Remember that financial recovery is a gradual process, and with patience and diligence, you can achieve your financial goals and secure your financial well-being.

11

Legal and Practical Considerations

Introduction:
Navigating the legal and practical aspects of divorce is a complex and often overwhelming task. In this chapter, we will explore important considerations, steps, and strategies to help you make informed decisions and protect your rights during the divorce process.

11.1 Legal Counsel:
Consider hiring an experienced divorce attorney to guide you through the legal process. A knowledgeable attorney can provide essential advice, protect your rights, and help you achieve a fair divorce settlement.

11.2 Legal Documentation:
Ensure that all legal documentation is accurate and up-to-date. Review and update your will, power of attorney, and any other legal documents to reflect your post-divorce wishes.

11.3 Understanding Your Rights:
Educate yourself about your legal rights and responsibilities in divorce. Understand how property division, child custody, alimony, and child support laws apply to your situation.

11.4 Mediation and Alternative Dispute Resolution:

Explore mediation or alternative dispute resolution methods as options for resolving divorce-related issues. These approaches can often lead to more amicable and cost-effective solutions than litigation.

11.5 Child Custody and Visitation:

Prioritize the best interests of your children when negotiating child custody and visitation arrangements. Aim for cooperative co-parenting solutions that provide stability and emotional support for your children.

11.6 Division of Assets and Debts:

Work with your attorney to ensure a fair and equitable division of marital assets and debts. Understand the value of your assets and consider long-term financial implications.

11.7 Child and Spousal Support:

If applicable, establish clear agreements for child support and alimony. Ensure that these arrangements comply with legal guidelines and address the financial needs of both parties and any children involved.

11.8 Updating Financial Accounts:

Update your financial accounts, including bank accounts, retirement accounts, and insurance policies, to reflect your post-divorce status and beneficiaries.

11.9 Consider Tax Implications:

Understand the tax implications of your divorce settlement, including potential changes in filing status, deductions, and capital gains. Consult with a tax professional for guidance.

11.10 Protecting Your Privacy:

Protect your personal information and privacy during and after divorce. Change passwords, update security settings, and consider adjusting your social media presence to maintain boundaries.

Conclusion:

Legal and practical considerations are crucial elements of the divorce process. By seeking legal counsel, understanding your rights, prioritizing the best interests of your children, and making informed decisions, you can navigate the legal and practical aspects of divorce more effectively. Remember that each divorce is unique, and working closely with professionals can help you achieve a resolution that aligns with your specific needs and circumstances.

12

Embracing a New Beginning: Thriving After Divorce

Introduction:
As you reach the final chapter of this guide, it's time to focus on the future and the opportunities that lie ahead. In this chapter, we will explore how to embrace a new beginning, find joy, and thrive after divorce.

12.1 Letting Go of the Past:
Begin by letting go of the past. While it's important to acknowledge your divorce and the emotions it brought, holding onto resentment or regrets can hinder your ability to move forward.

12.2 Self-Discovery:
Use this phase of your life as an opportunity for self-discovery. Reconnect with your interests, passions, and goals that may have been set aside during your marriage.

12.3 Building a Support Network:
Cultivate a strong support network of friends and loved ones who provide emotional support and companionship. Surrounding yourself with positive influences can boost your resilience.

12.4 Self-Care and Wellness:

Continue prioritizing self-care and wellness. Maintain healthy habits, both physical and emotional, to ensure your well-being and enhance your overall quality of life.

12.5 Setting New Goals:

Set new personal and professional goals that align with your values and aspirations. Having goals to work towards can provide a sense of purpose and motivation.

12.6 Embracing New Relationships:

If you choose to pursue new relationships, do so with an open heart and a clear understanding of your own wants and needs. Build connections based on shared values and mutual respect.

12.7 Practicing Gratitude:

Cultivate gratitude for the positive aspects of your life. Regularly reflecting on what you're thankful for can shift your perspective towards optimism and contentment.

12.8 Seeking Professional Help:

If you're struggling with emotional challenges or adjusting to post-divorce life, consider seeking the support of a therapist or counselor. Professional help can provide valuable guidance and coping strategies.

12.9 Forgiveness and Closure:

Work towards forgiveness and closure regarding your past marriage and divorce. Forgiveness is a powerful tool for releasing emotional baggage and embracing a fresh start.

12.10 Celebrating Your Growth:

Celebrate your personal growth and resilience. Recognize that you have the capacity to overcome challenges and create a fulfilling life after divorce.

Conclusion:

Embracing a new beginning after divorce is a transformative journey. By letting go of the past, nurturing self-discovery, building a strong support network, and prioritizing self-care, you can not only survive but thrive after divorce. Remember that your life is full of possibilities, and with resilience, self-compassion, and a positive outlook, you can create a joyful and fulfilling future.

www.ingramcontent.com/pod-product-compliance
Lightning Source LLC
Chambersburg PA
CBHW050209130526
44590CB00043B/3365